Words of Love

Copyright © 1977 Lion Publishing

Published by
Lion Publishing plc
Sandy Lane West, Oxford, England
ISBN 0 7459 1971 5 (paperback)
ISBN 0 7459 2105 1 (cased)
Albatross Books Pty Ltd
PO Box 320, Sutherland, NSW 2232, Australia
ISBN 0 7324 0253 0 (paperback)
ISBN 0 7324 0462 2 (cased)

First edition in this format 1991
Reprinted 1993, 1994

Photographs by Patricia and Charles Aithie - ffotograff.
Additional photographs by Neil Beer: page 13.

Quotations from *Good News Bible*, copyright 1966, 1971 and 1976 American
Bible Society; published by the Bible Societies and Collins.

Printed in Malaysia

◆ Words of ◆
LOVE

A LION BOOK

◆ GOD'S STEADFAST LOVE ◆

'The mountains and hills may crumble,
　　but my love for you will never end;
　　I will keep for ever my promise of peace.'
So says the Lord who loves you.

ISAIAH 54:10

◆ A LONG WAY FROM HOME ◆

Jesus said: 'There was once a man who had two sons. The younger one said to him, "Father, give me my share of the property now." So the man divided the property between his two sons.

'After a few days the younger son sold his part of the property and left home with the money.

'He went to a country far away, where he wasted his money in reckless living. He spent everything he had. Then a severe famine spread over that country, and he was left without a thing…

'At last he came to his senses and said, "All my father's hired workers have more than they can eat, and here I am about to starve! I will get up and go to my father and say 'Father, I have sinned against God and against you. I am no longer fit to be called your son; treat me as one of your hired workers.'" So he got up and started back to his father.

'He was still a long way from home when his father saw him; his heart was filled with pity, and he ran, threw his arms round his son, and kissed him.'

LUKE 15:11–20

✦ LOVE IS KIND ✦

I may have all knowledge and understand all secrets;
I may have all the faith needed to move mountains—
but if I have not love, I am nothing...

Love is patient and kind; it is not jealous or conceited
or proud; love is not ill-mannered or selfish or irrit-
able; love does not keep a record of wrongs; love is not
happy with evil, but is happy with the truth. Love
never gives up; and its faith, hope, and patience never
fail.

1 CORINTHIANS 13:2, 4–8

◆ LOVE YOUR NEIGHBOUR ◆

'Love the Lord your God with all your heart, with all your soul, and with all your mind.' This is the greatest and the most important commandment.

The second most important commandment is like it: 'Love your neighbour as you love yourself.'

MATTHEW 22:37–40

✦ THE GOOD SAMARITAN ✦

A teacher of the Law asked Jesus: 'Who is my neighbour?'

Jesus answered: 'There was once a man who was going down from Jerusalem to Jericho when robbers attacked him, stripped him, and beat him up, leaving him half dead.

'It so happened that a priest was going down that road; but when he saw the man, he walked on by, on the other side.

'In the same way a Levite also came along, went over and looked at the man, and then walked on by, on the other side.

'But a Samaritan who was travelling that way came upon the man, and when he saw him, his heart was filled with pity. He went over to him, poured oil and wine on his wounds and bandaged them; then he put the man on his own animal and took him to an inn, where he took care of him.

'The next day he took out two silver coins and gave them to the innkeeper. "Take care of him," he told the innkeeper, "and when I come back this way, I will pay you whatever else you spend on him."'

LUKE 10:29–35

◆ 'HIS LOVE IS ETERNAL' ◆

Give thanks to the Lord,
    because he is good;
    his love is eternal...

He alone performs great miracles;
    his love is eternal.
By his wisdom he made the heavens;
    his love is eternal;
he built the earth on the deep waters;
    his love is eternal.
He made the sun and the moon;
    his love is eternal;
the sun to rule over the day;
    his love is eternal;
the moon and stars to rule over the night;
    his love is eternal...

He did not forget us when we were defeated;
    his love is eternal;
he freed us from our enemies;
    his love is eternal.
He gives food to every living creature;
    his love is eternal.

Give thanks to the God of heaven;
    his love is eternal.

PSALM 136:1, 4–9, 23–26

◆ 'HE MAKES HIS SUN SHINE' ◆

You have heard that it was said,

'Love your friends, hate your enemies.'

But now I tell you: love your enemies and pray for those who persecute you, so that you may become the sons of your Father in heaven. For he makes his sun to shine on bad and good people alike, and gives rain to those who do good and to those who do evil. Why should God reward you if you love only the people who love you?

MATTHEW 5:43–46

✦ LOVE PAYS THE PRICE ✦

When they came to the place called 'The Skull', they crucified Jesus there, and the two criminals, one on his right and the other on his left.

Jesus said, 'Forgive them, Father! They don't know what they are doing.'

Standing close to Jesus' cross were his mother, his mother's sister, Mary the wife of Clopas, and Mary Magdalene.

Jesus saw his mother and the disciple he loved standing there; so he said to his mother, 'He is your son.'

Then he said to the disciple, 'She is your mother.' From that time the disciple took her to live in his home.

LUKE 23:33–34 ; JOHN 19:25–27

◆ PRAISE HIM ◆

I will tell of the Lord's unfailing love;
    I praise him for all he has done for us.
He has richly blessed the people of Israel
    because of his mercy and constant love.
The Lord said, 'They are my people;
    they will not deceive me.'
And so he saved them from all their suffering.

ISAIAH 63:7–9

◆ 'MY COMMANDMENT' ◆

My commandment is this: love one another, just as I love you. The greatest love a person can have for his friends is to give his life for them. And you are my friends if you do what I command you.

JOHN 15:12–14

◆ JESUS AND LAZARUS ◆

A man named Lazarus, who lived in Bethany, was ill. Bethany was the town where Mary and her sister Martha lived...

Jesus loved Martha and her sister and Lazarus. Yet when he received the news that Lazarus was ill, he stayed where he was for two more days. Then he said to his disciples, 'Let us go back to Judaea... Our friend Lazarus has fallen asleep, but I will go and wake him up.'

Jesus saw Mary weeping, and he saw how the people who were with her were weeping also; his heart was touched, and he was deeply moved.
'Where have you buried him?' he asked them.
'Come and see, Lord,' they answered.
Jesus wept.
'See how much he loved him,' the people said.

JOHN 11:1, 5, 11, 33–35

◆ LOVE AND DISCIPLINE ◆

When the Lord corrects you, my son, pay close attention and take it as a warning. The Lord corrects those he loves, as a father corrects a son of whom he is proud.

PROVERBS 3:11–12

◆ GOD SHARES HIS GLORY ◆

We know that in all things God works for good with those who love him, those whom he has called according to his purpose.

Those whom God had already chosen he also set apart to become like his Son, so that the Son would be the first among many brothers.

And so those whom God set apart, he called; and those he called, he put right with himself, and shared his glory with them.

ROMANS 8:28–30

✦ RAIN AND BLOSSOM ✦

I will bring my people back to me.
I will love them with all my heart;
    no longer am I angry with them.
I will be to the people of Israel
    like rain in a dry land.
They will blossom like flowers;
    they will be firmly rooted
    like the trees of Lebanon.
They will be alive with new growth,
    and beautiful like olive-trees.
They will be fragrant
    like the cedars of Lebanon.
Once again they will live under my protection.
They will flourish like a garden
    and be fruitful like a vineyard.
They will be as famous as the wine of Lebanon.

HOSEA 14:4–7

✦ LOVE DRIVES OUT FEAR ✦

We ourselves know and believe the love which God has for us.

God is love, and whoever lives in love lives in union with God and God lives in union with him. Love is made perfect in us in order that we may have courage on Judgement Day; and we will have it because our life in this world is the same as Christ's. There is no fear in love; perfect love drives out all fear. So then, love has not been made perfect in anyone who is afraid, because fear has to do with punishment.

We love because God first loved us.

1 JOHN 4:16–19

◆ LOVE–AND OBEY ◆

Whoever accepts my commandments and obeys them is the one who loves me. My Father will love whoever loves me; I too will love him and reveal myself to him...

Whoever loves me will obey my teaching. My Father will love him, and my Father and I will come to him and live with him. Whoever does not love me does not obey my teaching. And the teaching you have heard is not mine, but comes from the Father, who sent me.

JOHN 14:21, 23–24

• LOVE IN ACTION •

We know that we have left death and come over into life; we know it because we love our brothers.

Whoever does not love is still under the power of death. Whoever hates his brother is a murderer, and you know that a murderer has not got eternal life in him.

This is how we know what love is: Christ gave his life for us.

We too, then, ought to give our lives for our brothers! If a rich person sees his brother in need, yet closes his heart against his brother, how can he claim that he loves God?

My children, our love should not be just words and talk; it must be true love, which shows itself in action.

1 JOHN 3:14–18

◆ 'THERE WAS A WOMAN...' ◆

A Pharisee invited Jesus to have dinner with him, and Jesus went to his house and sat down to eat.

In that town was a woman who lived a sinful life. She heard that Jesus was eating in the Pharisee's house, so she brought an alabaster jar full of perfume and stood behind Jesus, by his feet, crying and wetting his feet with her tears. Then she dried his feet with her hair, kissed them, and poured the perfume on them.

When the Pharisee saw this, he said to himself, 'If this man really were a prophet, he would know who this woman is who is touching him...'

Jesus spoke up and said to him... 'There were two men who owed money to a moneylender...one owed him five hundred silver coins, and the other one fifty. Neither of them could pay him back, so he cancelled the debts of both. Which one, then, will love him more?'

LUKE 7:36–42

◆ LOVE ONE ANOTHER ◆

Dear friends, let us love one another, because love comes from God. Whoever loves is a child of God and knows God. Whoever does not love does not know God, for God is love.

And God showed his love for us by sending his only Son into the world, so that we might have life through him.

This is what love is: it is not that we have loved God, but that he loved us and sent his Son to be the means by which our sins our forgiven.

Dear friends, if this is how God loved us, then we should love one another. No one has ever seen God, but if we love one another, God lives in union with us, and his love is made perfect in us.

1 JOHN 4:7–12

• 'NOTHING CAN SEPARATE •
US FROM HIS LOVE'

Who, then, can separate us from the love of Christ?
Can trouble do it, or hardship or persecution or
hunger or poverty or danger or death? As the scripture
says,

'For your sake we are in danger of death at all times;
we are treated like sheep that are going to be
slaughtered.'

No, in all these things we have complete victory
through him who loved us! For I am certain that
nothing can separate us from his love: neither death
nor life, neither angels nor other heavenly rulers or
powers, neither the present nor the future, neither the
world above nor the world below—there is nothing in
all creation that will ever be able to separate us from
the love of God which is ours through Christ Jesus our
Lord.

ROMANS 8:35–39